Songkran

The Water Festival

It is Songkran.
Some people call this
the Water Festival.

Songkran is a time to think about new beginnings.

5

The children spray water on their friends.
They spray water in the street.

The elephants

spray water too.

Look at the sand.

The children will

take sand to the **temple**.

They will make the sand

into a **sand pagoda**.

Songkran is a time to give gifts.
The children are giving gifts to the **monks**.

13

Songkran is special for us.

15

Glossary

 monks

 sand pagoda

 temple